CHOCOLATE!

Contents

Chocolate and You	2
The History of Chocolate	4
The Production of Chocolate	8
Chocolate for Everyone!	14
Working with Chocolate	18

Recipes

Chocolate Milk	20
Hot Chocolate	20
Chocolate Milk Shake	21
Brownies	22
Fudge	24

When you see this symbol, ask an adult to help you.

Alternatives to Chocolate	26
Glossary	28
Index	29

Chocolate and You

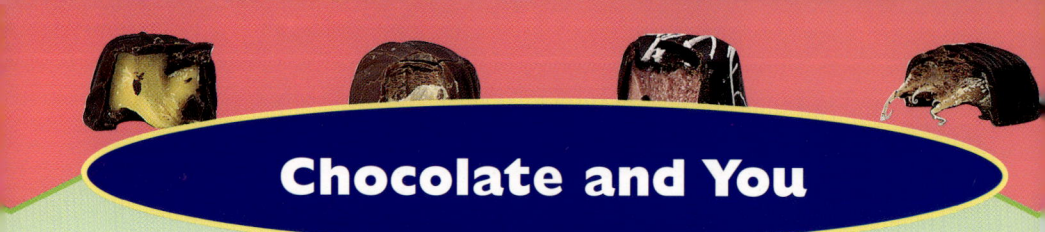

Most of us like chocolate even though we know that too much isn't good for us! Chocolate comes in many different forms, and it is eaten in most countries around the world. It is used in cooking, in drinks, and as a treat on special occasions.

Perhaps you have wondered where chocolate comes from and how it is made. Read on! This book will tell you all you want to know about chocolate.

POWDERED CHOCOLATE

DARK CHOCOLATE

WHITE CHOCOLATE

CHOCOLATE CHIPS

FILLED CHOCOLATES

FUDGE

Remember, knowledge is power. The more you know about chocolate, the more you'll enjoy eating it.

But don't be too tempted by the photographs. Chocolate is a treat, and too much of it simply is not good for you!

BAKING CHOCOLATE

SEMI-SWEET CHOCOLATE

COCOA

CHOCOLATE SYRUP

MILK CHOCOLATE

CHOCOLATE BARS

TRUFFLES

The History of Chocolate

Christopher Columbus is believed to have been the first European to taste chocolate. But by the time Columbus tried chocolate, it had been used for hundreds of years by the people of Central America.

The Maya harvested *cocoa beans* from *cacao trees*. They dried the beans, crushed them, and mixed them with hot water. This drink wasn't like the hot chocolate we drink. It was very bitter.

Chocolate Fact

The Aztecs used cocoa beans for money. They used the beans to purchase all sorts of goods, such as canoes (100 cocoa beans) and clothes. A feather cape cost 1,000 cocoa beans.

The Aztecs also grew cocoa beans. They crushed the beans and mixed them with cold water. Then they whipped the mixture until it was light and frothy. They mixed chili peppers and vanilla into the drink, too.

The Aztecs called this drink *xocoalt,* and only nobles were allowed to drink it. One Aztec emperor liked to drink his xocoalt out of a golden goblet. When he was finished, he would throw the goblet out the window, into a lake.

More on The History of Chocolate

In 1519, Hernando Cortez, a Spanish explorer, went to Central America. He made contact with the Aztecs, who invited him to feasts at which xocoalt was served.

When Cortez returned to Spain, he presented chocolate to the Spanish king. The king liked the drink, but felt it would taste better with sugar instead of peppers. And he wanted the drink served hot instead of cold. Modern hot chocolate was born!

Because Central America was far away, cocoa beans were in short supply in Spain. Only the king's court and very rich people could afford chocolate.

But it wasn't long before others heard about chocolate and demanded the treat be shared. Soon, word of chocolate spread to every city and every country.

Chocolate Fact

At first, not everyone liked chocolate. Some people said chocolate was good only for washing pigs, and when pirates raided ships, they sometimes just threw the bags of cocoa beans overboard!

The Production of Chocolate

All chocolate comes from the same place – the cacao tree. Cacao trees grow in Central America and in Africa, where the climate is always warm and humid.

These trees are evergreens and have large purple-and-white flowers that bloom from their trunks and branches. The flowers develop into the pods that hold the cocoa beans.

During the harvest, people cut down the ripe pods. They cut the pods in half and scoop out the beans and pulp inside.

The beans and pulp are placed out in the sun under banana leaves to dry and ferment. *Fermentation* takes away the bean's bitter taste. While drying, the beans turn from a dark purple to the familiar cocoa brown. After drying, the beans are placed in sacks and shipped to places all around the world.

Chocolate Fact

Cacao or cocoa? That is the question. The Latin name of the cacao tree — *Theobroma cacao* — means "food of the gods." But how does a cacao tree produce cocoa? Rumor has it that someone misspelled cacao as cocoa, and it caught on! Whatever the reason, cacao usually refers to the tree and pods, and cocoa refers to the beans and powder used in making chocolate.

More on The Production of Chocolate

1 Once the cocoa beans reach the factory, they are sorted according to size and then roasted in cylinders to bring out the full flavor of the beans. Then the shells are removed, exposing the *nibs,* the inside of the cocoa bean from which chocolate is made.

2 Next, the nibs are crushed. The high fat content, or *cocoa butter,* inside the nibs creates a liquid paste called *chocolate liquor.* It is from this liquid that all the basic types of chocolate are made.

The basic types of chocolate are *sweet* and *semi-sweet chocolate*, *baking chocolate*, *cocoa*, and *milk chocolate*.

Baking chocolate is unsweetened. It is made by cooling pure chocolate liquor.

Cocoa is usually in a powder form and is made by removing some of the fat content, or cocoa butter, from the pure chocolate liquor. The remaining liquor is dried and then ground into a fine powder.

Chocolate Fact

Nothing in the cocoa bean is wasted! Cocoa butter is used in the preparation of many skin creams, cosmetics, and sun screens. Cocoa bean shells are used for animal feed and fertilizers. Chemicals extracted from the cocoa beans are used to make many medicines and plastics.

Sweet and semi-sweet chocolate has sugar added, and is made much the same way as milk chocolate, but no milk is added.

More on The Production of Chocolate

3 Milk chocolate has a thickened sugar-and-milk mixture added to the chocolate liquor. After the mixtures have been combined and pressed together, the chocolate looks like a large crumbly cake.

4 Next, more cocoa butter is added, and the cake turns into a thick, lumpy chocolate paste. This paste is ground into a smooth mixture through a process called *conching*. A conching machine is a large vat with granite rollers. These rollers move back and forth through the milk chocolate mixture, breaking up the lumps. Sometimes, it takes three days to make the chocolate smooth and creamy.

5 Finally the milk chocolate is blended, pressed into molds, and cooled. Depending on the shape of the mold, the milk chocolate will become a bar shape or be cooled around cream, fruit, and nut centers to create filled candies.

Chocolate Fact

Sometimes, when chocolate is stored at temperatures over seventy degrees, the cocoa butter separates and comes to the surface, where it hardens into a white film. This is called *bloom*. It might not look very good, but the chocolate will still taste fine!

Chocolate for Everyone!

The first chocolate bar was created by chocolate makers J.S. Fry and Sons, but it tasted bitter, and wasn't very good. Milk chocolate was invented by two Swiss men named Jean Tobler and Henri Nestlé. They used powdered milk and sugar to make their chocolate. But it was very expensive.

Someone needed to make chocolate that everyone could afford. That someone was Milton Hershey!

At the Chicago's World Fair in 1893, Milton Hershey saw a machine that would allow him to make different kinds of chocolate, so he began to experiment.

One of Milton Hershey's experiments was to add sweetened condensed milk instead of powdered milk to the chocolate. This made the milk chocolate even tastier. Milton Hershey also found ways to make chocolate smoother and easier to make.

Chocolate Fact

Some researchers believe that there is a chemical in chocolate that is similar to the chemical your brain produces when you fall in love! But don't worry, eating chocolate won't make you fall in love with the first person you see!

When he felt he had it right, he built a factory that made so many chocolate bars, that their price was very low. He was so sure of his success, that he even built a town to go along with his factory: Hershey, Pennsylvania.

More on Chocolate for Everyone!

Now, mass-produced chocolate is available to just about everyone. We have many different kinds of chocolate for all sorts of occasions.

Chocolate is a sweet, delicious snack. It contains sugar, which provides quick energy. Hikers and endurance athletes often eat chocolate to get a quick boost. Soldiers are given chocolate rations in their field kits so that they can have a quick, easy energy snack.

Chocolate Fact

Nutrition Information

A 1.5 ounce (43 gram) chocolate bar contains:

Calories 230/Fat Calories 120
Total Fat   13 grams
Saturated Fat   9 grams
Cholesterol   10 milligrams
Total Carbohydrates   25 grams
Sugars   22 grams
Protein   3 grams

But too much chocolate isn't good for you. Cocoa butter is a fat, and chocolate has a lot of sugar. As shown by the food pyramid at the right, chocolate belongs to the least important food group – fats and sweets. You should eat plenty of breads, fruits and vegetables, and meat and dairy products before you indulge in chocolate.

Fats and sweets

Milk, cheese, and meat

Vegetables and fruits

Breads, cereal, rice, and pasta

17

Working with Chocolate

If you have ever left chocolate in a warm room or in a car on a hot day, you know what kind of sticky, runny mess it makes.

Since chocolate melts easily, and when cooled, hardens into a solid, you can mold it into different shapes and forms. And that's just what people do.

Chocolate Fact

Here are some jokes about chocolate:

What do you get when you cross a crocodile and a chocolate bar?
A chocodile

What do you get when you cover a moose with chocolate?
A chocolate mousse

What do you say if you fall into a vat of chocolate?
Nothing! Just open your mouth and start eating!

Chocolate is used to make many novelty items and candies. It is also used in baking, cooking, and drinks. On the following pages are recipes that use chocolate.

Chocolate Milk

Ingredients
Milk 16 ounces
Chocolate syrup 2 to 4 ounces

Utensils
Two tall glasses
Two long spoons

Method
Pour milk into glasses.
Pour chocolate syrup into glasses.
Stir until well mixed.

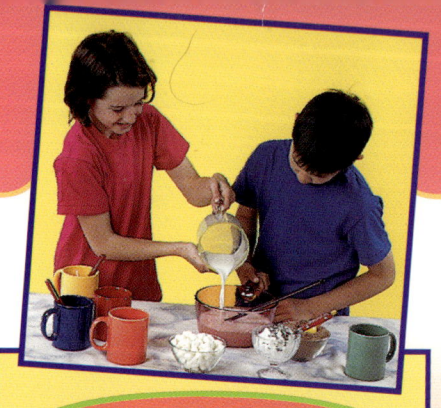

Hot Chocolate

Ingredients
Milk 16 ounces
Powdered chocolate 2 to 4 ounces
Marshmallows optional
Whipped cream optional

Utensils
Sauce pan
Cooking spoon
Two mugs

Method
Pour milk into sauce pan.
Heat milk on stove over low heat.
Add chocolate powder and stir until steam rises. Do not boil!
Pour into mugs.
Add marshmallows or whipped cream if desired.

Chocolate Milk Shake

Ingredients

Milk   16 ounces
Chocolate syrup   2 to 4 ounces
Ice cream   4 to 6 ounces

Utensils

Blender
Ice-cream scoop
Two parfait glasses
Straws

Method

Pour milk into blender.
Pour chocolate syrup into blender.
Scoop ice cream into blender.
Put lid on blender and blend
   mixture until smooth.
Pour shake into
   parfait glasses.

Brownies

Ingredients

Sugar	8 ounces
Shortening (butter or margarine)	4 ounces
Eggs	2
Cocoa	2 ounces
Flour	6 ounces
Baking powder	1/2 teaspoon
Salt	1/2 teaspoon
Vanilla	1/2 teaspoon
Nuts	4 ounces (optional)

Utensils

Mixing bowl
Spoon
Spatula
Measuring cup
Measuring spoons
8 x 8 x 2 baking pan

Method

Preheat oven to 350°.
Pour sugar into bowl, add shortening, and stir until mixed.
Add eggs and vanilla, and mix well.
Combine flour, baking powder, and salt, and add to bowl.
Add cocoa and mix well.
Stir in nuts if desired.
Lightly oil baking pan and pour in batter.
Bake at 350° for 30 to 35 minutes.
Cool and cut into 16 equal squares.

Fudge

Ingredients

Sugar	16 ounces
Milk	6 ounces
Cocoa	2 ounces
Corn syrup	2 tablespoons
Salt	1/4 teaspoon
Shortening (butter or margarine)	2 ounces
Vanilla	1 teaspoon
Nuts	4 ounces (optional)

Utensils

Sauce pan
Spoon
Spatula
Measuring cup
Measuring spoons
8 x 8 x 2 baking pan
Candy thermometer (optional)

Method

Pour sugar into pan.
Add milk.
Add cocoa, corn syrup, and salt, and stir until mixed.
Cook over a medium heat until mixture forms a soft ball when dropped in cold water, or reaches 234° on candy thermometer.
Remove from heat, add margarine, and stir until well mixed.
Cool mixture (120° on candy thermometer) and stir in vanilla.
Stir in nuts if desired.
Pour mixture into baking pan.
Cool until firm, then cut into 16 equal squares.

Alternatives to Chocolate

Some people are allergic to chocolate, while others wish to avoid the high fat and sugar content of most chocolate candies. *Carob* is the most common substitute for chocolate and is produced from the gum of the carob tree. The gum is roasted and ground into a chocolate-like powder that can be used in candies and for baking and cooking.

On the next page is a recipe for fudge that uses carob instead of chocolate.

Carob Fudge

Ingredients

Honey	8 ounces
Peanut Butter	8 ounces
Carob	8 ounces
Sunflower seeds (shelled, unsalted)	8 ounces
Sesame seeds	4 ounces
Coconut	4 ounces
Pecans (shelled, broken)	4 ounces
Raisins	4 ounces

Utensils

Sauce pan
Spoon
Spatula
Measuring cup
Measuring spoons
8 x 8 x 2 baking pan

Method

Put honey and peanut butter into pan.
Cook over a low heat and stir until mixture is smooth.
Remove from heat and stir in remaining ingredients until mixed.
Pour mixture into baking pan.
Cool until firm, then cut into 16 equal squares.

Glossary

Baking chocolate – A bitter chocolate made from pure unsweetened chocolate liquor and used in cooking and baking

Bloom – Term given to the white film of cocoa butter that sometimes covers chocolate after it has been stored in a warm place

Cacao tree – The evergreen tree from which cocoa beans are obtained

Carob – A chocolate substitute made from the gum of the carob tree

Chocolate liquor – The liquid paste obtained from crushing the nibs of the cocoa bean and used as the basis for all chocolate

Cocoa – A powder made from chocolate liquor that has had a portion of cocoa butter removed and is used for hot chocolate drinks and baking

Cocoa bean – The bean from the seed pods of the cacao tree

Cocoa butter – The fat content of the cocoa bean that is added to or removed from various forms of chocolate and also used in skin creams, cosmetics, and sun screens

Conching – A process in which milk chocolate is mixed by granite rollers to remove lumps and make the chocolate smooth and creamy

Fermentation – The process in which cocoa beans lose their bitter taste and turn from purple to brown

Milk chocolate – Chocolate that has had sugar, milk, and extra cocoa butter added and is used in chocolate bars and other candies

Nibs – The center of the cocoa bean that is ground into chocolate liquor

Sweet and semi-sweet chocolate – Two kinds of chocolate that have been sweetened with sugar and are used for candies and baking

Theobroma cacao – Literally "food of the gods," the scientific name for the cacao tree

Xocoalt – The Aztec name for the drink created from crushed cocoa beans, water, peppers, and vanilla

Index

Aztecs	4, 5, 6	conching	12
baking chocolate	11	Cortez, Hernando	6
bloom	13	fermentation	9
brownies	22–23	Fry, J.S.	14
cacao tree	4, 8–9	fudge	24–25
carob	26	Hershey, Milton	14–15
carob fudge	27	Hershey, Pennsylvania	15
carob tree	26	hot chocolate	4, 6, 20
chocolate bar	14, 15, 17	Maya	4
chocolate liquor	10, 11, 12	milk chocolate	11, 12–13, 14, 15
chocolate milk	20	Nestlé, Henri	14
chocolate milk shake	21	nibs	10
cocoa	11	sweet and semi-sweet chocolate	11
cocoa bean	4, 5, 7, 9, 10, 11	*Theobroma cacao*	9
cocoa butter	10, 11, 12, 13, 17	Tobler, Jean	14
Columbus, Christopher	4	xocoalt	5, 6

Author

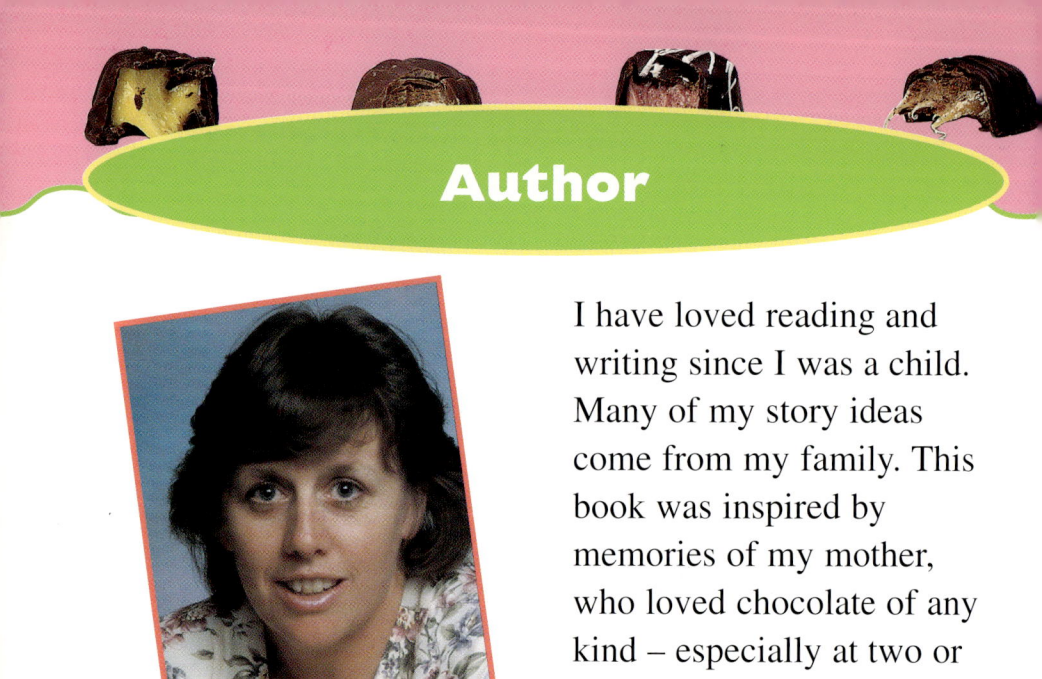

I have loved reading and writing since I was a child. Many of my story ideas come from my family. This book was inspired by memories of my mother, who loved chocolate of any kind – especially at two or three o'clock in the morning!

Linda Velarde

Illustrator

I was born in Toledo, Ohio, in 1954. Besides illustrating children's books and magazine articles, I also enjoy hang gliding, snowshoeing, and playing bingo.

Ralph Whirly

Photographer

I live in Denver with my wife, my daughter, and our dog, and work as a photographer for our local newspaper. I enjoy working with young people, playing basketball with my daughter, and being creative.

John Sunderland

SOMETHING STRANGE
My Father the Mad Professor
A Theft in Time: Timedetectors II
CD and the Giant Cat
Chocolate!
White Elephants and Yellow Jackets
Dream Boat

ANOTHER TIME, ANOTHER PLACE
Cloudcatcher
Flags
The Dinosaur Connection
Myth or Mystery?
Where Did the Maya Go?
The Journal: Dear Future II

WHEN THINGS GO WRONG
The Long Walk Home
The Trouble with Patrick
The Kids from Quiller's Bend
Laughter Is the Best Medicine
Wild Horses
The Sunday Horse

CONFIDENCE AND COURAGE
Imagine This, James Robert
Follow That Spy!
Who Will Look Out for Danny?
Fuzz and the Glass Eye
Bald Eagles
Cottle Street

Written by **Linda Velarde**
Photographed by **John Sunderland**
Illustrated by **Ralph Whirly**
Edited by **David Nuss**
Designed by **Pat Madorin**

Additional photography by **Ant Photo Library:** Frithfoto (cacao pods, p. 8); **Austral International:** (cocoa beans, p. 8; split cacao pod, p. 9); **Chocolate Manufacturers Association:** (pp. 10-13)

© 1997 Shortland Publications Limited
All rights reserved.

02 01 00 99 98 97
10 9 8 7 6 5 4 3 2 1

Distributed in the United States by
   Rigby
   a division of Reed Elsevier Inc.
   P.O. Box 797
   Crystal Lake, IL 60039-0797

Printed by Colorcraft, Hong Kong
ISBN: 1-57257-738-X